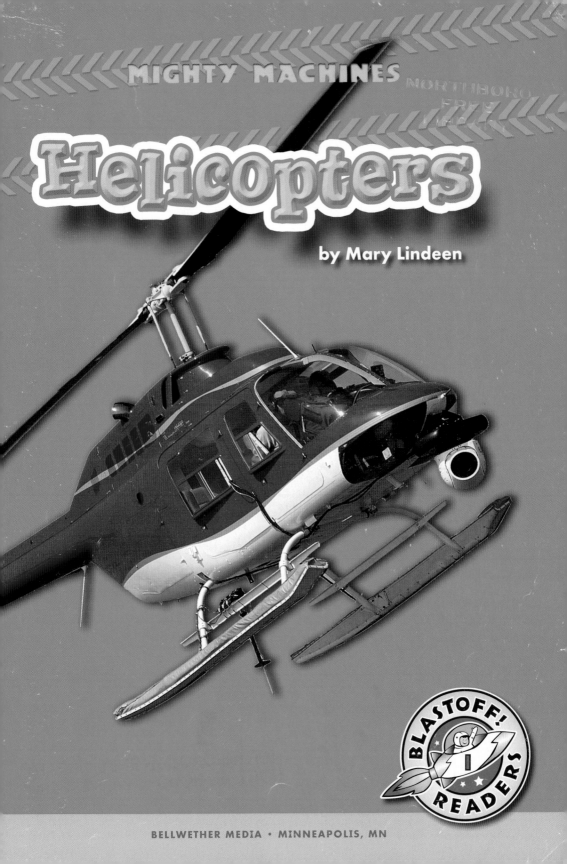

MIGHTY MACHINES

Helicopters

by Mary Lindeen

BLASTOFF! READERS

BELLWETHER MEDIA • MINNEAPOLIS, MN

Note to Librarians, Teachers, and Parents:

Blastoff! Readers are carefully developed by literacy experts and combine standards-based content with developmentally-appropriate text.

Level 1 provides the most support through repetition of high-frequency words, light text, predictable sentence patterns, and strong visual support.

Level 2 offers early readers a bit more challenge through varied simple sentences, increased text load, and less repetition of high frequency words.

Level 3 advances early-fluent readers toward fluency through increased text and concept load, less reliance on visuals, longer sentences, and more literary language.

Level 4 builds reading stamina by providing more text per page, increased use of punctuation, greater variation in sentence patterns, and increasingly challenging vocabulary.

Level 5 encourages children to move from "learning to read" to "reading to learn" by providing even more text, varied writing styles, and less familiar topics.

Whichever book is right for your reader, Blastoff! Readers are the perfect books to build confidence and encourage a love of reading that will last a lifetime!

This edition first published in 2008 by Bellwether Media.

No part of this publication may be reproduced in whole or in part without written permission of the publisher. For information regarding permission, write to Bellwether Media Inc., Attention: Permissions Department, Post Office Box 1C, Minnetonka, MN 55345-9998.

Library of Congress Cataloging-in-Publication Data
Lindeen, Mary.
  Helicopters / by Mary Lindeen.
    p. cm. — (Blastoff! readers) (Mighty machines)
Summary: "Simple text and supportive images introduce young readers to Helicopters. Intended for students in kindergarten through third grade."—Provided by publisher.
  Includes bibliographical references and index.
  ISBN-13: 978-1-60014-119-5 (hardcover : alk. paper)
  ISBN-10: 1-60014-119-6 (hardcover : alk. paper)
  1. Helicopters—Juvenile literature. I. Title.

TL716.2.L56 2008
629.133'352—dc22
                                         2007009769

Contents

A helicopter
is a flying
machine.

A helicopter
has two
rotors.
One is on
top and one
is on the tail.

rotors

Rotors spin fast. The top rotor lifts the helicopter up into the air.

A pilot steers
by moving a
control stick.

**control
stick**

A helicopter can take off or land in very small spaces. It lands on parts called **skids**.

skids

13

A helicopter can **hover** in one place. This one hovers while it **rescues** people from a **flood**.

This air ambulance helicopter carries sick people to the hospital.

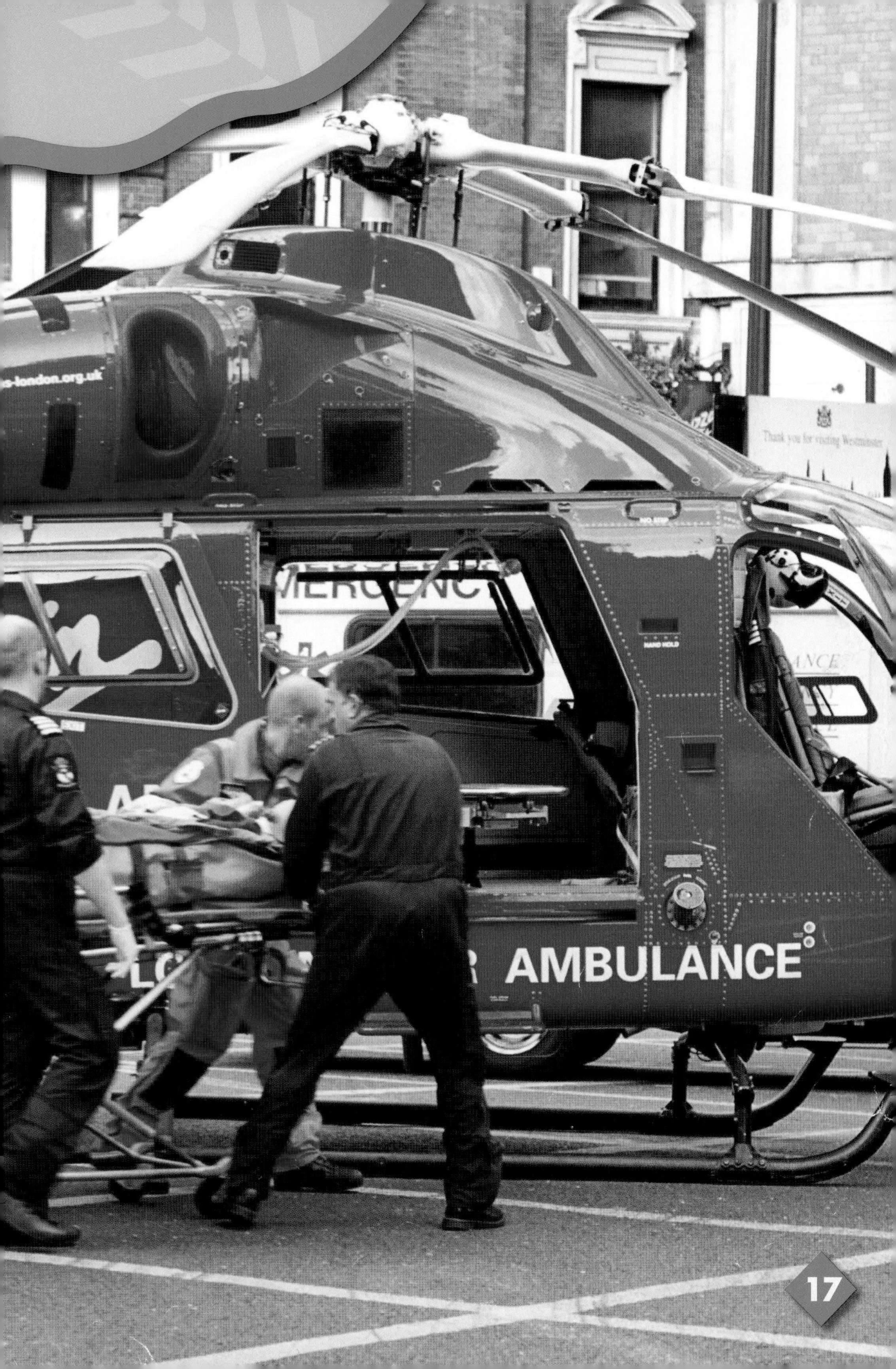
AMBULANCE
Thank you for visiting Westminster

This
helicopter
fights fires.

This helicopter
takes people
for a fun ride.
What a view!

Glossary

control stick—a stick used to steer or direct a machine

flood—when water rises and spreads over the land

hover—to stay in one place in the air

rescue—to save someone who is in danger

rotors—the blades of a helicopter; the top rotor lifts the helicopter in the air while the back rotor helps control the direction that the helicopter flies.

skids—runners on the bottom of a helicopter; a helicopter rests on skids when it is on the ground.

To Learn More

AT THE LIBRARY

Anderson, Joan. *Harry's Helicopter*. New York: William Morrow, 1990.

Englart, Mindi Rose. *Helicopters*. San Diego, Calif.: Blackbirch, 2003.

Zuehlke, Jeffrey. *Helicopters*. Minneapolis, Minn.: Lerner, 2004.

ON THE WEB

Learning more about mighty machines is as easy as 1, 2, 3.

1. Go to www.factsurfer.com

2. Enter "mighty machines" into search box.

3. Click the "Surf" button and you will see a list of related web sites.

With factsurfer.com, finding more information is just a click away.

Index

The photographs in this book are reproduced through the courtesy of: Stas Volik, front cover; Bruce C. Murray, p. 5; Stas Volik, p. 7; Jon Shireman/Getty Images, p. 9; Ivan Cholakov, p. 11; Juan Martinez, p. 13; David J. Phillip/Associated Press, p. 15; don jon red/Alamy, p. 17; A. T. Willett/Alamy, p. 19; Mark Kelly/Getty Images, p. 21.